CUPCAKES AT WORK

An ABC Book

by
Ulrike Scheuchl

www.ulrikescheuchl.com

Copyright © 2017 by Ulrike Scheuchl

All rights reserved.

ISBN: 978-1545473863

To my nieces and nephews,
whom I encourage to pursue their dreams.

If you think cupcakes are lazy, think again!
See what they can do.

Abby the **a**stronaut

Bill the builder

Charlotte the chemist

Dorian the dressmaker

Emma the executive

Finn the firefighter

Grace the gardener

Hannah the hairdresser

Isabel the illustrator

Jordan the journalist

Kate the kindergarten teacher

Logan the lifeguard

Mike the mechanic

Nora the nurse

Oscar the oil painter

Paige the **p**olice officer

Quinn the quilter

Riley, Robin, and Ryan the rock stars

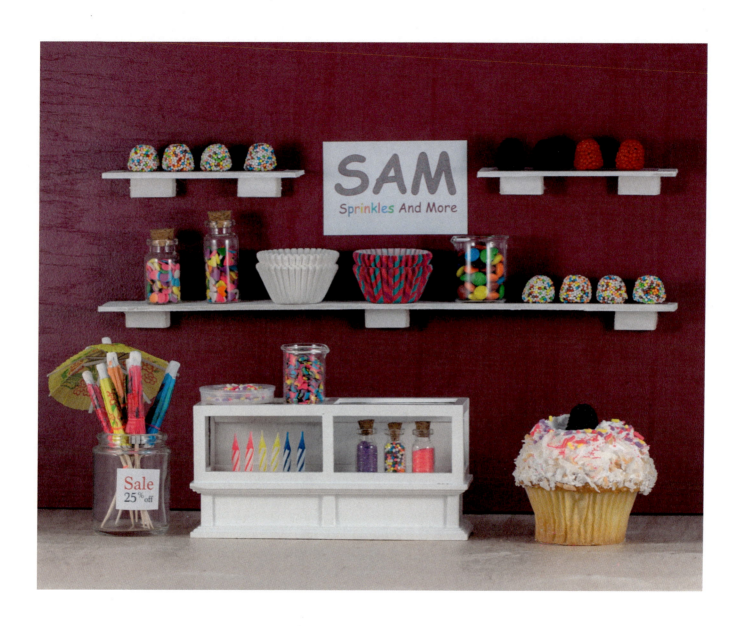

Sam the shopkeeper

Taylor the teacher

Ursula the **u**pholsterer

Vivian the veterinarian

Willow the waitress

Xavier the x-ray technician

Yara the yoga teacher

Zoe the **z**ookeeper

ABOUT THE ARTIST

Ulrike Scheuchl, originally from Austria, now lives in Laguna Beach, California. *Cupcakes at Work* is her third book, after *The Secret Life of Cupcakes* and *C. C. Cupcake Explores the Southwest*. Ulrike gained valuable skills from her previous work experience in e-commerce and human resources before embracing her passion for art and photography.

www.ulrikescheuchl.com

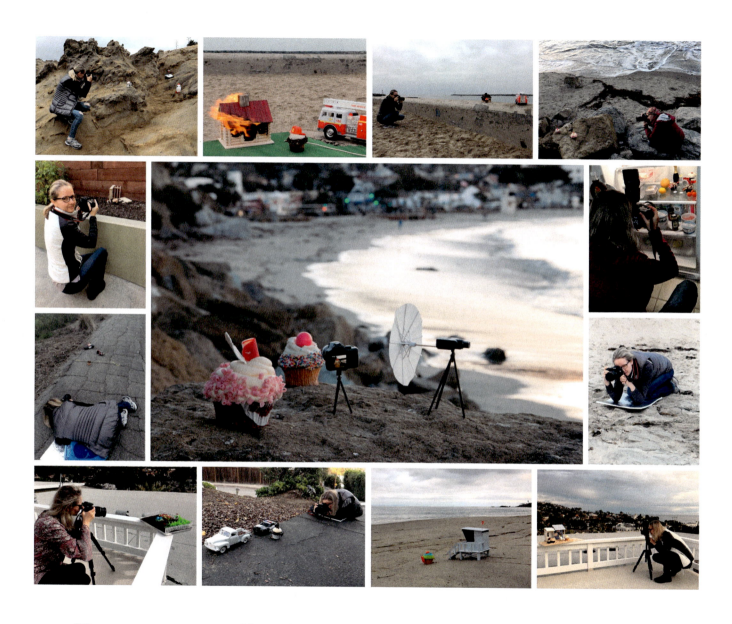

If you see someone taking pictures of cupcakes in and around Laguna Beach, it is most likely Ulrike, the unconventional photographer.

ACKNOWLEDGMENTS

I would like to thank the following contributors:

All cupcakes and their creators for making life a little sweeter.

Juliette, Arthur, Celine, Renee, and Christian for providing me with props.

Karin, Laura, Debra, and Sandra for their feedback.

My parents and in-laws for their support throughout my career.

Prop master and beloved husband, Bernd, without whom this book would not have been possible.

And you, dear reader, for being my biggest motivation.